D0486007

The
World's Best
After-Dinner
Jokes

The World's Best After-Dinner Jokes

Edward Phillips

Illustrations by Graham Morris

HarperCollins*Publishers*

HarperCollinsPublishers
77–85 Fulham Palace Road,
Hammersmith, London W6 8JB

A Paperback Original 1993
3 5 7 9 8 6 4

Text copyright © Edward Phillips 1993
Illustrations copyright © Graham Morris 1993

A catalogue record for this book is available
from the British Library

ISBN 0 00 637960 5

Set in Goudy Old Style by
Avocet Typesetters, Bicester, Oxon

Printed in Great Britain by
HarperCollinsManufacturing Glasgow

The proud young mother was discussing with her husband what they should call the new baby. 'I've made up my mind,' she declared firmly. 'We'll call her Penelope.' The husband didn't like the name at all, but he decided to be subtle about it.

'That's a lovely name, dear,' he said. 'The first girl I ever went out with was called Penelope and it will bring back pleasant memories.'

'I think we'll call her Mary, after my mother,' said the wife.

A businessman decided to take the afternoon off and got home about three o'clock in the afternoon. The house was quiet and he went upstairs and opened the bedroom door. His wife was in bed and there was a strange man lying on top of her with his head between her breasts. 'What the hell are you doing?' he shouted.

The man looked up and said, 'I'm listening to the music.'

'What music?' said the husband, and he leaned over and put his ear to his wife's chest. 'I can't hear any music,' he said suspiciously.

'Of course you can't,' said the stranger. 'You're not plugged in.'

A schoolteacher asked her class to write an essay on the subject of the Police. One boy's essay consisted of just three words: 'Police is bastards.'

The teacher was, naturally, shocked, and she arranged for her class to visit the local police station so that they could meet the policemen and find out how they worked. The police were most co-operative and the children had a great day out, listening in to the radio calls, riding around in panda cars and inspecting the police station, the whole thing topped off with a slap-up tea.

Back at school the next day, the teacher again asked the class to write an essay on the police, based on their experiences. This time the lad's essay consisted of the following: 'Police is cunning bastards.'

A prominent City banker fell in love with an actress and for several weeks, he took her out and about to all the fashionable nightclubs and restaurants. Deciding to ask her to marry him, he prudently engaged a firm of private detectives to check her antecedents, since any hint of scandal might jeopardize his position in the City.

In due course, he received their report: 'Miss Delamere appears to have led a blameless existence, and there are no indications of promiscuity, drugs, or criminal activities. Her friends and acquaintances are similarly beyond reproach. The only thing we have been able to discover about her is that, in recent weeks, she has been seen around in the company of a City banker of doubtful reputation.'

A suburbanite rang up a friend of his to invite him to a party. 'You know the address, don't you?' he said. 'You can't miss it – when you get to the town hall, take the second turning on the left, and we're the fourth house along. Just ring the bell with your elbow.'

'Why my elbow?' said his friend.

'Well, you're not coming empty-handed, are you?' he said.

The club bore was talking about his travels in India. 'I remember on one occasion,' he said, 'in a little village on the banks of the Ganges, a number of the women were washing clothes when a large tiger appeared from nowhere. One of the women immediately splashed some water in its face, and do you know, that tiger turned round and slunk back into the jungle!'

There was a moment's silence and then another club member said, 'I can vouch for the truth of that incident. I was there myself. As I was coming down to the river, I came face to face with the tiger and I stroked its whiskers. Gentlemen, those whiskers were wet!'

A doting mother, who wanted desperately to see her 23-year-old daughter happily married, decided to help matters along by putting an advertisement in the local paper. After careful consideration, she submitted the following to the Lonely Hearts Column: *Lonely, unattached red-head, 23, good figure, fun-loving, uninhibited, seeks male company.*

A few days later, the daughter asked her mother whether there had been any replies. 'Just one,' said her mother grimly. 'From your father!'

The cute little secretary walked into her boss's office one morning and said, 'I have some good news and some bad news for you.'

'Look, I'm very busy this morning,' said the boss. 'Just tell me the good news.'

'Well,' said the secretary, 'the good news is that you're not sterile.'

The hotel lobby was crowded as the receptionist shouted, 'Is there a Mr Hausenburgenkranzermacher here? I have an urgent message for Mr Hausenburgenkranzermacher.'

A bespectacled gent looked up from his newspaper and said, 'What initial?'

At the weekly meeting of the Women's Institute, one of the members was enthusing about the recent First Aid course she had attended. 'It was a lucky thing I went on that course,' she said. 'I was coming down the High Street yesterday when I heard a big crash behind me. I looked round and there was this poor chap who'd been knocked down by a taxi. He was covered in blood, and he looked to have a broken arm and a compound fracture of the leg – and possibly a fractured skull. And then I remembered what I had learned on my First Aid course. So I bent over and put my head between my legs to stop myself from fainting.'

Shortly after the German invasion of Belgium in 1940, a Panzer regiment occupied a small town near the frontier. The commanding officer of the German troops assembled all the inhabitants in the town hall and instructed them to take an oath of allegiance to the Third Reich. One man refused indignantly and boasted of the brave defence the Belgian army had put up against the invading Nazi hordes. The German was outraged and shouted, 'Unless you take this oath of allegiance, you will be taken outside and shot!'

Bowing to the inevitable, the Belgian took the oath and

the officer said, 'That's better! Now you are one of us!'

The Belgian looked at him and said, 'Fine! But didn't those Belgians give us a hell of a fight!'

Two ex-army men met in a pub and began to talk over old times in the service. 'You remember I used to be in the band?' said one. 'Well, I used to play the trumpet, and I married a girl who plays the piano. We've got two children – a boy who plays the drums, and a girl who's a dab hand with the guitar. Tell you what – pop over one evening and we'll give you a little musical concert.'

'I'll do that,' said his pal. 'I used to box for the regiment and I married a girl who's got a black belt at judo. My boy's a policeman and does a bit of wrestling on the side. You must come round to us one evening – we can't give you a musical concert but we'll give you a bloody good hiding!'

Groucho Marx was leaving a particularly boring Hollywood party. At the door, he said to the hostess, 'I've had a wonderful evening – but this wasn't it.'

A man went to see his solicitor and asked if he could have his wife traced. They had been married twenty-five years ago and had split up just three days after the wedding. The solicitor asked him why he had waited so long – was he thinking of a divorce? 'No,' said the man. 'I just thought we might get together to celebrate our Silver Anniversary.'

A woman went to a psychiatrist and said, 'It's my husband, doctor. He thinks he's a lift.'

'Well, why don't you ask him to call in and see me?' said the psychiatrist.

'He can't,' said the wife. 'He doesn't stop at this floor.'

'What happened?' asked the hospital visitor of the heavily bandaged man sitting up in bed.

'Well, I went down to Margate at the weekend and decided to take a ride on the roller coaster. As we came up to the top of the highest loop, I noticed a little sign by the side of the track. I tried to read it but it was very small and I couldn't make it out. I was so curious that I decided to go round again, but we went by so quickly that I couldn't see what the sign said. By now, I was determined to read that sign so I went round a third time. As we reached the top, I stood up in the car to get a better view.'

'And did you manage to see what the sign said this time?' asked the visitor.

'Yes.'

'What did it say?'

'Don't stand up in the car!'

A holiday-maker wrote to a hotel in Devon asking if it was all right for his dog to stay there too. The hotel owner wrote back: *Dear Sir, I have been running this hotel for fifteen years. Never once in all that time has a dog set the bedclothes on fire by smoking in bed. I have never found hotel towels in a dog's suitcase, or had a dog attempt to pass off a bad cheque on me. Your dog is welcome – and if he can vouch for you, you can come too.*

Arthur Sullivan, of Gilbert and Sullivan fame, was reputed to have perfect pitch. One night, he stumbled home after a late party, considerably the worse for drink. He had difficulty in identifying his house from all the other identical houses in the street so he went down the row kicking at the metal shoe-scrapers by the side of each flight of steps. Eventually he came to one and kicked it, then paused and kicked it again. 'Ah! E flat!' he muttered. 'This must be the one.'

A young married couple were having a furious argument. 'I wish now that I'd taken my mother's advice and never married you!' sobbed the bride.

'Do you mean to tell me,' said the husband incredulously, 'that your mother tried to stop you marrying me?'

'Yes, she did,' said the wife.

'Good God!' the husband exclaimed. 'How I've wronged that woman!'

A woman went to her doctor for a check-up and he said, 'You've been married three times, haven't you?'

'Yes,' she said.

'And yet you're still a virgin?' said the doctor.

'Yes,' she replied. 'You see, my first husband was a homosexual. My second was ninety-three years old. And my third was in public relations. All he did was sit on my bed and tell me how wonderful it was going to be.'

A fellow on a Mediterranean cruise was invited by the captain to take a look around the bridge. 'This is a first-class ship,' the captain told him. 'The crew are all hand-picked. Every man is an expert at his job. You see that fellow down there, swabbing the deck? He's a typical example. I would trust that man with my life.' Just then a huge wave dashed over the ship and swept the sailor overboard.

'You know that feller you said you'd trust with your life?' said the passenger. 'Well, he's just done a bunk with your mop and bucket!'

A woman rang up a vet in the small hours and complained that a dog and a bitch were copulating noisily at the bottom of her garden. Could he do anything about it? 'Madam,' said the vet, 'it's half past two in the morning and you've got me out of bed. Why don't you try telling those dogs that they're wanted on the phone?'

'Do you think that will stop them?' asked the woman.

'Well, it certainly stopped me,' said the vet.

An old lady from the West Country had reached her hundredth birthday and was being interviewed on television. 'You look in remarkably good health,' said the interviewer. 'Have you ever been bedridden?'

'Oh, yes,' she answered. 'Lots of times. And once in a hansom cab!'

A Dublin lawyer was defending a client who was being sued for returning a borrowed lawn mower in a damaged condition. 'Your Honour,' said the lawyer, 'we refute this charge on the following grounds. In the first place, my client never borrowed the lawn mower at all. In the second place, it was already damaged when he borrowed it. And in the third place, it was in perfect condition when he returned it.'

Two friends were chatting in the saloon bar and one said, 'No matter what kind of girl I bring home to meet my parents, my mother disapproves of her.'

'I'll tell you what to do,' said his friend. 'Find a girl just like your mother. She's bound to like her.'

A week later, the two friends met again. 'Did you do what I advised?' asked the second fellow.

'Yes, I did,' replied the first. 'I found a girl who was just like my mother – even dressed and talked like her.'

'So what happened when you took her home?'

'My father hated her!'

Orson Welles was once lecturing in a small town in Kansas. Only a handful of people turned up to hear him and he looked round at the half-dozen people in the audience and said, 'My name is Orson Welles. I am an actor, a writer, a director and a producer. I am also a painter and a magician, and I play the piano and the violin. Isn't it a pity there are so many of me and so few of you!'

A prospective parliamentary candidate had just finished a long speech in the local hall of a small town in the north of England. Feeling very pleased with himself for having delivered a rousing, fact-filled and inspiring speech, he said, 'Are there any questions?'

'Yes,' said a bored voice from the back. 'Who else is running?'

George Bernard Shaw once sent Winston Churchill a couple of tickets for the opening night of one of his plays. Attached to the tickets was a note: *Bring a friend — if you have one.*

Churchill was busy that evening, so he returned the tickets to Shaw with a note which read: *Can't make tonight. I'll come to the second performance — if there is one.*

A millionaire businessman once commissioned a French artist to paint his wife's picture. At the first sitting, the wife said to the Frenchman, 'I know I am not a great beauty, and I would like a true likeness, but please, Monsieur, may I ask that you paint me with sympathy.'

After some weeks the portrait was finished and the husband arranged a grand unveiling ceremony. The cover was drawn back from the portrait and the assembled guests gasped in horror. It was a wonderful likeness but the picture showed a man's hand reaching into the lady's bosom. The husband was furious. 'How dare you insult my wife in this fashion!' he stormed.

'But, Monsieur, I do not understand,' protested the

Frenchman. 'Your wife asked me to paint her with sympathy. I did not know what "sympathy" meant so I looked it up in the dictionary. It said, "Sympathy – a fellow feeling in your bosom." '

An Irishman was fishing when suddenly he heard a voice from overhead. 'There are no fish under the ice!' the voice boomed.

The Irishman dropped his rod in a panic and said in a trembling voice, 'Is that you, God?'

'No,' thundered the voice. 'I'm the manager of the ice rink!'

A psychiatrist interviewing a patient said, 'I want to try some free association. Just answer the following questions as quickly as you can – just say the first thing that comes into your head. Now, first – what is it that a man does standing up, a lady sitting down, and a dog on three legs?'

'Shakes hands,' said the patient at once.

'Good,' said the psychiatrist. 'Now what is it that a dog does in the garden that you wouldn't want to step in?'

'Digs a hole,' said the patient without hesitation.

'Right,' said the psychiatrist. 'And, finally, what is it that sticks stiffly out of your pyjamas when you wake up in the morning?'

'Your head,' said the patient.

'Excellent,' said the psychiatrist. 'Your responses are perfectly normal – but you'd be surprised at some of the weird answers I get!'

An American was complaining to an Englishman in the Savoy Grill that he found many English terms confusing. 'You say "rubbish" and we say "garbage",' he explained. 'We say "elevator" and you say "lift"; you say "dustbin" and we say "trash can". And then there's your pronunciation – I can't make head or tail of that.'

'Surely that shouldn't give you any problems?' said the Englishman. 'There can't be that much difference.'

'Oh yeah?' said the American. 'Why, only the other day, I was walking down Drury Lane and I passed a theatre with a big sign saying, "CATS – pronounced success!"'

A man on a Caribbean cruise was standing on the deck one night, admiring the moonlit waters, when another passenger approached, pulled out a small container from his pocket, and sprinkled the contents over the water. 'Those are my wife's ashes,' he explained.

'I see,' said the first man. 'You must have loved her very much.'

'No,' said the second man. 'I hate fish.'

A very devout rabbi, deeply engrossed in his meditations, had a vision in which he imagined that he saw God himself. 'You look worried,' said God. 'Is anything the matter?'

'Oh, God, it's my son,' the rabbi said. 'He's about to become a Christian!'

And God said, '*Your* son!'

A mother took her three-year-old son to a psychiatrist and explained that she was worried that he was becoming too precocious. 'Right,' said the psychiatrist, 'we'll try a few simple tests.' Turning to the boy, he said, 'Just say a few words – anything that comes into your mind.'

The boy turned to his mother and said, 'Does he want logically constructed sentences or just random and purely isolated words?'

A young lady approached a gentleman at a Mayfair party and said, 'Do you remember me? A few years ago, you asked me to marry you.'

'And did I?' replied the man.

An Irish detective arrested a wanted criminal in a Dublin street. Just as he was about to slap the handcuffs on him, a gust of wind blew the detective's hat down the street. 'Shall I go and fetch it for you?' asked the criminal.

'Do you think I'm crazy?' said the detective. 'You wait here and I'll go and get it.'

A visitor to an Indian reservation in Oklahoma met a Comanche chief on the top of a mountain. The chief was squatting by a small fire and sending out smoke signals. Having an interest in Indian customs, the visitor asked, 'How big a fire do you usually build?'

'Well,' said the Indian, 'that depends on whether it's a local or a long-distance call.'

An examiner marking papers at Cambridge came across the following answer to one of the mathematics questions: 'God only knows the answer to this one.' He returned the paper with the notation: 'God gets an A. You get an F.'

'Doctor,' said the patient, 'I had a peculiar dream last night. I dreamed you were my mother.'
'So?' said the psychiatrist. 'What happened?'
'Nothing – I woke up.'
'And then?'
'I had breakfast.'
'And what did you have for breakfast?'
'Oh, just a piece of toast and a cup of coffee.'
'Call that a breakfast?' said the psychiatrist.

At the height of his popularity, Rudyard Kipling was earning quite a lot of money. An American admirer once wrote to him, saying, 'They tell me that you get $1 a word from your writing. I enclose a dollar for which please send me a sample.'
Kipling replied. 'Thanks.'
Soon afterwards, he received another letter from the American: 'I sold the "Thanks" anecdote for $2. Enclosed pleased find 45 cents being half the profits from the transaction, less postage.'

An English tourist arrived in Cairo. As soon as he set foot on Egyptian soil, a pimp came up to him and said, 'You want nice little virgin, nine years old?'

'Of course not!' said the visitor.

'How about very pretty little boy, ten years old, also virgin?'

'Get away from here!' said the tourist, outraged. 'I don't want a little girl or a little boy! I want the British Consul!'

'Hmmm,' murmured the pimp. 'Very difficult – but I try.'

On a visit to Brighton, a lady went into a fortune-teller's tent. After the customary crossing of the palm with silver, the clairvoyant said, 'I see a bright future for you. You will meet a tall, dark, handsome man. He will be very rich. You will marry him and he will take you off to a life of luxury. You will have everything your heart desires.'

'Sounds great,' said the lady. 'Just one question . . .'

'Ask away,' said the fortune-teller.

'How do I get rid of my husband?'

A young girl visiting Paris was propositioned by a Frenchman and eventually succumbed to his advances. She was very surprised, however, when he insisted on having her against a wall instead of in bed. Afterwards, she asked him why. 'All Frenchmen know,' he explained, 'that the English are always at their best when their backs are against the wall.'

An Irish disc jockey was introducing a record. 'This next one,' he said, 'is for Mr Michael O'Reilly, who is a hundred and eleven. Well done, Michael, that's a ripe old age, isn't it!' There was a short pause, and then the disc jockey said, 'I'm sorry, I got that wrong. This next record is for Michael O'Reilly, who is ill.'

The visitor was complaining to the landlady. 'Your advertisement claimed that your hotel was only ten minutes from the sea,' he said. 'It took me forty-five minutes to get there this morning.'

'Ah,' said the landlady, 'you've been walking. We don't cater for pedestrians.'

Some people seem to be phenomenally unlucky. Like the young unmarried girl who one day found herself pregnant. Wishing to avoid a scandal in the rather strait-laced community in which she lived, she announced that she was going off on holiday. She travelled to another city at the other end of the country and registered in a small private hospital using a false name. She didn't write home or telephone or tell any of her friends or family where she was. And then she gave birth to quintuplets.

A fellow came ashore outside Calais having swum the Channel in record time. There was a big crowd waiting to greet him and one of the Frenchmen said, 'Magnifique! You 'ave performed the great foot!'

'You mean "feat", don't you?' said the swimmer.

'Mon Dieu!' exclaimed the Frenchman. 'You 'ave swum both ways?'

Two fellows met in the pub and one said, 'What's the matter with you?'

'My aunt's just died,' said his friend.

'But I thought you didn't like her,' said the first fellow.

'I didn't, but it was through me that she spent the last five years of her life in a mental institution. She's left all her money to me and now I've got to prove she was of sound mind.'

A little old lady phoned the Fire Brigade and told them her kitchen was on fire. 'Right,' said the fireman taking the call. 'How do we get there?'

'Don't you have your little red fire-engine any more?' queried the lady.

A small boy in the East End of London had been away from school for a couple of days. On his return, his teacher asked him where he had been. 'My Dad got burnt,' he said.

'Oh, I am sorry,' said the teacher. 'Was it serious?'

And the boy answered, 'Well, they don't muck about at the crematorium, miss!'

In a little village in northern Italy, the priest was addressing the villagers in the local church. 'You must not use-a the Pill!' he exhorted.

A young signorina stepped forward and said indignantly, 'Hey! You no play-a da game, you no make-a da rules!'

When British Rail were planning their new route from central London to the coast, they wrote to a farmer advising him that the proposed line would run right through the middle of his barn. They offered him very good compensation amounting to ten times as much as the property was worth, so it came as something of a shock to his wife when he turned the offer down. 'It's a good offer!' she exclaimed. 'Why don't you take it?'

'No!' he said. 'Do you think I'm going to keep running out to that barn day and night to open and shut the door every time they want to run a train through it?'

A young lady went into Boston's most exclusive department store and made her way to the Ladies' Fashions department. She tried on several dresses and each time, she slipped the dress on, sat down, separated her legs, and said, 'This won't do.' The middle-aged saleswoman was rather shocked and complained to the floor manager. He came over and told the young lady that perhaps it might be better if she left. The young lady said coldly, 'Sir, you have just insulted the principal cellist of the Boston Symphony Orchestra!'

The War Office recently received delivery of a brand-new computer, incorporating the very latest technological improvements. The Commander-in-Chief Home Forces arranged a tactical defence exercise in order to test the computer's capabilities. All the information about our forces and the enemy's was fed into the machine and then the C-in-C asked, 'How do I start the exercise, Computer? Do I attack or do I fight a defensive action?'

The computer replied, 'Yes.'

'Yes, what?' the C-in-C asked impatiently.

'Yes, *sir*!' said the computer.

It was the beginning of term at a primary school in South London. The teacher asked one little Indian boy his name and he replied, 'Ravashanka Vankatarataam Bannerjee.'

'How do you spell that?' she asked.

'My mother helps me,' said the boy.

A young lad obtained a job at a petrol station, wiping windscreens and generally helping out. One day, a very flash Mercedes pulled in, driven by a world-class golf pro. The driver went inside to make a telephone call, and while the young lad was cleaning the car windows he noticed some golf tees on the top of the dashboard. He knew absolutely nothing about golf, so when the pro returned, he asked him what they were for. 'They're to put my balls on when I'm driving,' said the pro.

'Blimey!' said the kid. 'These Mercedes people think of everything, don't they!'

At an Officer's Initiative Course at Sandhurst, the question was put to one group: 'Your platoon is under attack and the situation is desperate. Suddenly, one of the men panics, drops his rifle and runs past you to the rear. The other men look at you in despair. What action would you take?'

One of the officers wrote: 'I would shout "Henderson, hurry back with that ammunition!" '

One Sunday morning, Mark Twain attended a service at which the sermon was preached by Dr Doane, Bishop of Albany. At the end of the service, Twain said, 'A good sermon, Doctor, but you know, I have a book at home which contains every word of it.'

'Impossible!' said the Doctor. 'If there really is such a book, I would very much like to see it.'

The next day, Twain sent him a copy of a dictionary.

Two old ladies were making their very first flight in Concorde. As the stewardess came round to ask if there was anything they wanted, one of the ladies said, 'Please ask the pilot not to travel faster than sound. We want to talk.'

At a recent auction at Sotheby's, the auctioneer said, 'I must interrupt the sale for a moment, gentlemen. A buyer has lost a wallet containing £5,000. He has offered a reward of £300 for its return.'

And a voice from the back of the room shouted, '£350!'

'**D**id you have a good day at the office, dear?' asked the young wife.

'No,' replied the husband. 'The computer broke down and we all had to think.'

A well-known actress complained to a photographer the pictures he had taken of her made her look too old, and weren't half as good as the ones he had taken some years earlier. 'You must remember,' he explained, 'that I am ten years older than I was on the last occasion I worked for you.'

During the recent Gulf War, a fellow seeking a bit of adventure went into an army recruiting office to sign up. The recruiting officer said, 'What experience do you have? Do you have any war records?'

'Yes, as a matter of fact, I've got two,' said the fellow. 'A Gracie Fields and a Vera Lynn.'

British Rail have a report form that must be completed whenever there is an incident on the line. On one occasion, a driver was filling out the form after accidentally killing a cow on the tracks. In the section devoted to accidents of this kind, there was a section marked 'Disposition of Carcass'. After considerable thought, he wrote: 'Kind and gentle.'

Adam noticed that the animals were often wandering off into the forest in pairs and re-emerging some time later with contented smiles on their faces. He asked Eve about it and she said, 'Don't you know? It's called reproduction.'

The next time he spoke to God, Adam asked, 'What's reproduction?'

'Why don't you take Eve into the woods and find out,' said the Lord.

Adam tried this, but the next time he spoke to God, he asked, 'Lord – what's a headache?'

There was a big murder trial in Iceland recently. At one point, counsel for the prosecution is alleged to have asked a witness, 'Will you please tell the court where you were on the night of the 10th of November to the 6th of March.'

Little Johnny disgraced himself at the dinner table by announcing loudly that he was going for a wee-wee. 'Don't say that, Johnny,' said his shocked mother. 'In future, if you want to go to the toilet, try to be more discreet. Just say, "I want to whisper." '

The next day, little Johnny's grandfather came for a visit. That night at dinner, as Granddad was drinking his soup, Johnny said, 'Excuse me, Granddad – I want to whisper.'

'All right,' said Granddad. 'Come over here and whisper in my ear.'

A small boy accompanied his parents to a nudist colony. They all stripped off and went out into the garden. The boy looked around with interest and then asked his father why 'some men had big ones and some had small ones'. Dad couldn't be bothered with long explanations so he just said, 'Those with big ones are smart and those with small ones are stupid.'

The boy wandered off on his own for a while and then met his father again. 'Have you seen your mother?' asked Dad.

'She's behind that bush over there,' said the boy, 'talking to a stupid man who's getting smarter by the minute.'

The following is the text of a letter said to have been received by an income tax official in Nigeria:

DEAR SIR,

With reference to the attached form. I do not know what is meant by filling in this form. I am not interested in this income service. Please cancel my name in your books as this system has upset my mind and I do not know who registered me as one of your customers.

The lady of the manor at a large stately home in Lincolnshire wrote to the commander of a nearby American air base inviting him to send a dozen airmen round to afternoon tea. She added a PS: 'Please don't send any Jews.'

On the appointed afternoon, her door-bell rang promptly at four o'clock. She opened the door to find twelve black airmen standing on the steps. 'Oh!' she said in confusion, 'there must be some mistake!'

'No, ma'am,' said the airman in charge of the party. 'Captain Cohen never makes mistakes.'

A very keen amateur gardener was very proud of his ferns, the fronds of which were particularly fine specimens. He decided to try his hand at anemones but the results were a disaster. He complained to his friend. 'My fronds are absolute perfection,' he said, 'but I just can't grow anemones.'

'Never mind,' replied his friend. 'With fronds like these, who needs anemones!'

A young girl whose job it was to sell cosmetics by telephone, called one number and when a male voice answered, asked to speak to his wife. 'I'm afraid my wife is dying and can't speak to anyone,' replied the man sadly.

'Oh, I am sorry,' said the girl.

And the voice replied, 'So am I. I wanted her to stay brunette.'

A fellow was cleaning out his attic one morning when he came across an old brass lamp. He gave it a rub and a genie appeared in a puff of smoke. 'I am the genie of the lamp,' said the apparition. 'For releasing me, I will answer any three questions you care to ask.'

'Who? Me?' said the young man.

'Yes, you,' replied the genie. 'Now, what's your third question?'

'It seems there were these two Jews . . .' a comedian said as he started his routine in a northern club.

Immediately, a fellow stood up and shouted, 'Just a minute! I'm Jewish – why are you always knocking Jewish people like this? Every other joke you hear these days starts off "There were these two Jews . . ." '

'Sorry,' said the comedian. 'No need to take offence. I'll start again. There were these two Chinese, Lee Chan and Fu Ching, on their way over to the synagogue for a barmitzvah . . .'

'I'm sorry,' said the gynaecologist, after completing his examination, 'but removing that vibrator is going to involve a very delicate operation.

'Well,' said the young lady, 'couldn't you just change the batteries?'

During a naval exercise in the Mediterranean, a signaller rushed up to the bridge and said, 'Captain, this message just came in.'

'Read it out,' said the captain.

'Well, sir, I . . .' the signalman stammered.

'Just read it out – now!' snapped the captain.

'Right, sir,' said the signalman. 'It reads: *What the hell do you think you're doing, you stupid, blundering idiot? You're not fit to be in command!*'

'Yes, well . . .' said the captain. 'Have that decoded at once.'

An MP decided to take up ballooning. On his first trip, the weather took a turn for the worse and the balloon was forced down into a field miles from anywhere. As the mist closed in, the MP realized that he was completely lost. Just then, he noticed a farmer crossing the field and he shouted, 'Can you tell me where I am?'

'You're in a balloon!' the farmer shouted back, and carried on walking.

Recounting this incident to his colleagues in the bar of the House of Commons the next day, the MP said, 'That farmer gave me the perfect parliamentary reply. It was short. It was true. And it gave absolutely no new information.'

Two married couples made up a foursome for an evening of contract bridge. One of the husbands was a terrible player and his wife became progressively more annoyed as they lost hand after hand. Eventually, the husband excused himself to go to the bathroom, and his wife remarked, 'This is the first time all evening that I know what he has in his hand.'

Having finished his dinner, a man was leaving a West End restaurant. The owner of the restaurant was standing in the doorway, and as the man passed him a solid silver sugar bowl slipped out from under his bulging jacket and dropped to the floor with a resounding crash. With great presence of mind, the man looked round and said indignantly, 'Who threw that?'

A famous violinist became very interested in the effect of classical music on wild animals. He went out to Africa and took his violin into the heart of the jungle. Then he took out his violin and started to play a beautiful piece by Paganini. A huge gorilla approached and sat down entranced. He was followed by a fierce-looking bull elephant and a twenty-foot boa constrictor, both of whom stopped to listen to the music with dreamy expressions on their faces. Soon the violinist was surrounded by a group of normally ferocious animals, all listening, fascinated, to the music. Then an old lion bounded up, leaped on the violinist and tore him to pieces. 'What the hell did you do that for?' cried the gorilla. 'Our first chance to listen to really good music and you go and ruin it!'

And the lion cupped his paw to his ear and said, 'Pardon?'

The vicar of a small parish in a West Country town had a horseshoe hanging over his front door. 'I'm surprised to see a horseshoe up there,' said one of his parishioners. 'I didn't know you believed in these pagan superstitions. Do you really think it will bring you luck?'

'No, I'm not really superstitious,' said the vicar. 'But I have been told that it works even if you don't believe in it.'

The school governor was addressing a class of sixth-form girls at the end of the school year. 'Now, remember, girls,' he said, 'you are the mothers and wives of tomorrow!'

'It was through getting things in that order,' muttered the headmistress, 'that we had to expel Susie Simpkins!'

Two Irish astronauts landed on the moon and one of them left the spaceship to take a walk round the lunar landscape, leaving the other one to prepare for the journey home. After about half an hour, there was a knock on the door of the spaceship. The second astronaut looked up and said, 'Who's there?'

A woman went into a butcher's shop to buy a chicken. The butcher produced the last chicken he had for sale that day and the woman said, 'Have you got one a little bigger?'

'Just a minute,' said the butcher and he disappeared with the chicken into the back room, where he plumped up the bird so that it looked bigger. Returning into the shop, he put it down on the counter and said, 'How about this?'

'Fine,' said the woman. 'I'll take both of them.'

A honeymoon couple entered the lift at their hotel. As the lift ascended, one of the other guests, a very attractive young girl, looked at the groom and said, 'Hello, darling!'

When they reached their bedroom, the new bride said icily, 'And just who was that in the lift?'

'Don't you start!' said the groom. 'I'll have enough trouble explaining you to her!'

A little boy returning home from his first day at school said to his mother, 'Mum, what's sex?' His mother, who believed in all the most modern educational theories, gave him a detailed explanation, covering all aspects of the tricky subject. When she had finished, the little lad produced an enrolment form which he had brought home from school and said, 'Yes, but how am I going to get all that into this one little square?'

A woman whose husband had just joined the Navy attended church one Sunday morning. She only just got there in time and she hurriedly handed the vicar a note, asking if he would read it out in the pulpit. The note read: *Norman Smith having gone to sea, his wife desires the prayers of the congregation for his safety.*

The minister, in a hurry, took the note and went up into the pulpit. When the time came for him to read the notices, he glanced quickly at the note and said, 'Norman Smith, having gone to see his wife, desires the prayers of the congregation for his safety.'

The local church was putting on a nativity play and the vicar went up to London to order a banner from a firm of printers. Unfortunately he lost the note he had made of the dimensions of the banner and the Bible quotation to be printed on it, so he sent a fax message to his wife, asking her to confirm the details. He went out to lunch whilst awaiting the reply and when this came through it was taken by one of the clerks in the printing firm. The poor girl nearly fainted when she read the message: *Unto us a child is born — eight feet long and three feet wide.*

An East End trader who euphemistically described himself as being in 'imports and exports' fell foul of the Inland Revenue and was summoned for an interview. 'It seems from our records,' said the inspector, 'that you have not filed any returns for eight years. According to our calculations, you owe a total of £30,000 in back taxes, and I must request immediate payment, otherwise we shall have to issue the usual summons.'

'That's fair enough,' said the trader, and he opened a large suitcase which he had with him, and produced £30,000 in used notes.

The surprised tax man counted the money and said, 'Well, that seems to be in order – I'll just give you a receipt.'

'A receipt!' gasped the trader. 'Thirty thousand nicker in cash and you're going to put it through the books!'

The great chess master Bobby Fischer was travelling through the southern states of America and booked in one night at a small town in the backwoods of Alabama. The proprietor had no idea who he was and asked him in the course of the evening if he would like to play a game of chess. Being Fischer, he did not reveal his identity, but agreed to play. To his amazement, the hotel proprietor wiped the floor with him in seventeen moves – and without using his rooks. 'This is incredible!' Fischer said. 'And you never even used your rooks!'

'Oh, you mean those pieces at each end shaped like little castles?' said the hotel proprietor. 'No – I never did figure out how they moved.'

A door-to-door salesman knocked at the door of a typical suburban house in Wimbledon. 'Good morning,' he said. 'Would you care to buy a copy of *Five Hundred Excuses To Give Your Wife For Staying Out Late?*'

'Why on earth would I want a book like that?' said the lady of the house.

'Because,' replied the salesman, 'I sold a copy to your husband at his office this morning.'

An Irishman, an Italian and a Jew were regaling each other with stories about how they were continually being mistaken for famous historical figures. 'Oh, yes,' said the Irishman. 'Why I was walking through the park the other day and a fellow shouted "Morning, Saint Patrick!" '

The Italian said, 'I was standing on the street corner yesterday and a man passed by and said, "Hello, Mussolini!" '

The Jew said, 'That's nothing. I was walking through the park this morning and a policeman shouted, "Jesus Christ, get off the grass!" '

A fellow staying at a seaside boarding house sat down to dinner on his first evening and the dog growled at him. 'What's the matter with him?' the fellow asked.

'You've got his plate,' said the landlady.

'Well, I hope he makes friends,' said the guest nervously.

'So do I,' said the landlady. 'You're sleeping with him tonight.'

A fellow received a 'Second Notice' from the tax authorities informing him that his tax payment was overdue and threatening legal action if settlement was not immediately forthcoming. He hurried down to the collector's office and wrote out a cheque, saying, 'I would have paid you before but I didn't get your First Notice.'

'Oh,' said the clerk, 'we've run out of First Notices – and anyway, we find that the Second Notices are far more effective.'

The headmaster of a school in South London asked the father of one of his pupils to pop in for a chat. When the father arrived in his office, the headmaster said, 'I'm afraid this is serious. It's about your son, Jimmy.'

'What's he been up to now?' asked the father.

'Well, yesterday, we caught him having a wee in the swimming pool.'

'Well, that's not so bad, is it?' said the father. 'All little boys have an occasional wee in the swimming pool.'

'I know,' said the headmaster. 'But not from the top diving board!'

A professor of biology was lecturing to his class on the subject of cause and effect. He placed a flea on the desk in front of him and ordered it to jump. The flea jumped. Then he picked the flea up and cut off its legs. Placing it back on the desk, he again ordered it to jump. The flea didn't move. 'This demonstrates conclusively,' he said, 'that when the legs of a flea are removed, it is rendered completely deaf.'

A young husband came home from the office one evening and found his wife in tears. 'Darling, the most terrible thing has happened!' she sobbed. 'The first casserole I ever made for you and the cat ate it!'

'Don't worry, darling,' said the husband. 'I'll get you another cat tomorrow.'

It was a teenage marriage. The groom was seventeen. The bride was sixteen, going on pregnant. When the vicar asked the bridegroom to repeat after him: 'With all my worldly goods I thee endow,' the groom's mother turned to her husband and whispered, 'There goes his paper round!'

The Germans had just occupied Paris, and on the day of their arrival, a young French girl was raped by a German soldier. Afterwards, he said to her, 'In nine months, you will have a son – you may call him Adolf.'

She replied, 'In nine days, you will have a rash – you may call it measles.'

A lovely young thing was walking down the King's Road in Chelsea, wearing the tightest pair of jeans you ever saw. A young man approached her and said, 'I hope you don't mind my asking, but how on earth does anyone get into those pants?'

'Well,' she said, 'you could start by buying me a Martini.'

A young married couple decided it would be a good idea if they made their wills. Returning from the solicitor's office, the husband said, 'I'm glad we did that, darling. If anything happened to me, I'd want you to get married again. I only ask one thing: if you did, don't let him wear my clothes.'

'Oh, no,' replied the wife. 'Anyway, they wouldn't fit him.'

F ather had decided that the time had come when he should explain the facts of life to his teenage son. He called the lad into his living-room one morning and spent the next hour explaining in great detail everything he knew of the sexual process. Utterly exhausted, and not wishing to go through the whole business again with his younger son, he said, 'Now, David, can I rely on you to explain everything to Michael?'

'Sure, Dad,' said the teenager. 'Leave it to me.'

That afternoon, David took Michael aside and said, 'Micky, I had a long lecture from Dad this morning and he wants me to pass on to you everything he told me. You remember what you and I were doing with those girls behind the bicycle shed at school the other week? Well, Dad wants me to tell you that the birds and the bees do it too.'

A prize bull was on display at an agricultural show. It was kept in a special enclosure and there was a charge of £1 per person to see the mighty beast. A man with twelve children took his whole family along and the ticket attendant said, 'Are all these children yours?'

'They are,' said the man.

'Well, you wait here a minute,' said the attendant, 'and I'll bring the bull out to see you.'

A newly married couple were spending their honeymoon in Rio de Janeiro. One morning, they bought a brightly coloured parrot and took it back to their hotel room. However, the bird kept up a running commentary on their love-making and after a few days of this, the annoyed groom flung a blanket over its cage and shouted, 'If I hear one more word out of you, I'm taking you down to the zoo and leaving you there!'

On the last day of the honeymoon, the couple were packing their clothes away prior to departure. They had bought so many souvenirs that they had great difficulty in closing the last suitcase. They decided that one of them should stand on it while the other attempted to fasten it. 'Darling,' said the groom, 'you get on top and I'll try.' This proved unsuccessful, so the groom said, 'Wait a minute – I'll get on top and you try.' This didn't work either, so the groom said, 'Look, darling, let's both get on top and try.'

At this point, the parrot whipped the blanket off its cage and squawked, 'Zoo or no zoo, this I've got to see!'

Deep in the heart of Morocco, a sheikh decided to set off on a trip across the desert. He was short of a horse, so two of the villagers were ordered to bring their horses to his tent so that he could choose the best one to take. Neither of the villagers wanted to give up his horse and both protested that their steeds were worthless. 'We'll have a race,' said the sheikh. 'I will take the winner.'

'But, sire,' said one of the sheikh's advisers, 'neither man will let his horse go fast.'

'Yes, they will,' replied the sheikh. 'Let each man ride the other's horse.'

A fellow visited Las Vegas and lost all his money at the tables. He didn't even have enough money left to go to the toilet and he was obliged to borrow a coin from another patron of the gaming rooms. When he got to the toilets, however, another fellow was just coming out of one of the cubicles. Holding the door open, this fellow said, 'Here you are — use this one.'

Returning to the tables afterwards, our hero used the coin to play a slot-machine — and won. With his winnings, he went back to the roulette table and by the end of the evening he had won a considerable fortune.

Rich and famous, he went round the country lecturing on his experiences, and declaring that if he ever met his benefactor, he would split his winnings with him. In one audience, a man at the back of the hall jumped up and shouted, 'I'm the man who gave you the coin!'

'You're not the one I'm looking for,' said the lucky winner. 'I'm looking for the man who left the door open!'

A s the bombs fell on London in 1941, the city hospital was being evacuated. Matron was hastily going through her desk drawers. 'Doctor!' she shouted to the Chief Surgeon, 'I can't find my teeth!'

'Never mind about that!' the surgeon shouted back. 'It's bombs they're dropping — not sandwiches!'

A country vicar in a small parish in the West Country had one serious failing — he could never remember names. Whenever he had any announcement to make, he had to write all the names down on a sheet of paper. One morning he delivered a funeral sermon that went something like this: 'Dearly beloved, we are gathered here today to pay tribute to [glancing at his notes] Albert Jones, a man who came here to [glancing at his notes] Shepton Mallett thirty years ago and soon became one of us. He married a local girl [glancing at his notes] Betty Hardcastle, and settled down to raise a family, two fine boys [glancing at his notes], Michael and David. And now at last, after a long and happy life, he rests in the bosom of Our Saviour [glancing at his notes], Jesus Christ!'

A Frenchman came over to London to visit some English friends. He was invited to a neighbour's Silver Wedding Anniversary, a celebration that he knew nothing about. 'What ees this Silvair Wedding?' he asked.

'Well,' said his host, 'it means that Derek and Connie have been living together for twenty-five years.'

'Ah, I see!' said the Frenchman. 'And now they get married! *Formidable!*'

When Pope John Paul II took over the papacy, he caused a certain amount of consternation one Easter. As part of the Easter celebrations, it was the custom for the Chief Rabbi of Rome to enter the Basilica and present the Pope with an ancient scroll. Every year, the Pope would take this scroll, bow to the Rabbi, and hand it back unopened. This ceremony had been going on for centuries and no one could even remember what it signified. The new Pope decided to put an end to this ritual and to the horror of the assembled cardinals, when the scroll was handed to him, he opened it up. It was a bill for the Last Supper.

A n old farmer went to his doctor for a medical examination. His doctor had told him to bring a specimen with him, and he handed over a large bottle which was almost full. The doctor examined the sample and then said, 'Excellent – nothing wrong with that at all.'

When he got home some time later, the farmer said to his wife, 'Good news, dear. Neither you nor I, nor the kids, nor grandpa and grandma, nor the horse have a thing the matter with us!'

A fellow was taking a walk in the country when he came upon a large house with a notice by the front door which read: PLEASE RING BELL FOR THE CARETAKER. He rang the bell and an elderly man opened the door. 'Are you the caretaker?' he asked.

'Yes,' said the old man. 'What do you want?'

'I just wondered why you can't ring the bell yourself.'

C alvin Coolidge, President of the United States (1923–1929), was noted for being a man of very few words. At a White House press conference, one of the reporters asked him whether he had any comments to make about Prohibition. 'No,' replied Coolidge.

'Have you anything to say about the agricultural situation?' asked another reporter.

'No,' said Coolidge.

'What about the forthcoming senatorial campaign – have you anything to say about that?' asked another press man.

'No,' said Coolidge. As the reporters began to file out of the room, he called after them, 'And don't quote me.'

There was once a fellow who was sent for psychiatric treatment because he was suffering from delusions. He was firmly convinced that he would shortly receive a letter that would make him rich. The letter would be from a firm of solicitors telling him that a distant relative had died and left him a vast estate in Scotland and a priceless collection of art and antiques. The psychiatrist worked very hard over a period of months to cure him of this delusion. And just when he had the man cured, the letter arrived.

A survey on sexual habits was being carried out by a popular newspaper and one questioner stopped an elderly Italian gentleman in the street who was wearing a black suit and asked him how often he had sexual intercourse. 'Oh, about half a dozen times a year,' said the gentleman. The questioner smiled.

'I thought you Italians were supposed to be sexy,' she said.

'We are,' said the gentleman. 'But I don't think half a dozen times a year is so bad for a seventy-two-year-old priest with no car.'

'Well, Jimmy,' said the proud father, 'how did your first riding lesson go?'

'Great, Dad,' said Jimmy. 'I made friends with the horse and I even gave him a drink of water.' Dad smiled.

'I think you're supposed to say you watered the horse,' he said.

'Am I?' said Jimmy. 'All right. I watered the horse. And now I'm going to milk the cat.'

Suzanne the maid was leaving to get married. 'I'm very pleased for you, Suzanne,' said her mistress. 'You will have it much easier now that you're getting married.'

'Yes, madam,' said Suzanne. 'And more frequently I hope.'

Mark Twain used to receive a large number of photographs from men who thought they looked like him. Twain got fed up with answering these letters so he had a form letter printed which read:

DEAR SIR,
Thank you very much for your letter and photograph. In my opinion you are more like me than any other of my numerous doubles. I may even say that you resemble me more closely than I do myself. In fact, I intend to use your picture to shave by.

A farmer's wife went to the chemist to pick up two bottles of medicine. 'Now you be sure to label those bottles clearly,' she said. 'I must know which one is for the horse and which one is for my husband. I don't want nothing to happen to that horse before we get the spring ploughing done!'

There was a report in the newspapers recently about a man who got married so many times, he married one of his ex-wives without realizing it. He never would have known but for the fact that he recognized his mother-in-law.

At a recent lecture on sexual habits, the lecturer said that sex could be regarded as a form of communication. A member of the audience stood up and asked, 'Does that mean that masturbation is sort of like talking to yourself?'

The office manager was completely bald. Naturally, he was continually being teased by the other members of the staff and he was becoming increasingly irritated. One morning, a brash young executive ran his hand across the manager's bald pate and said, 'Do you know, this feels just like my wife's bottom!'

The manager ran his own hand across his bald scalp and said, 'You're right. It does!'

A Balkan peasant was riding through the forest one sunny morning in the early years of this century. He pulled his horse up just in time to avoid treading on a frog. But this

was no ordinary frog. This was a magic frog, and as a reward for saving its life, it granted the peasant three wishes. The peasant said that he would like to be extremely rich, of royal birth, and married to a beautiful young girl.

There was a blinding flash, a puff of smoke, and the peasant found himself lying in a magnificent four-poster bed, under a royal coat-of-arms. Beside him was a beautiful young girl in a silken nightdress. 'Hurry up, Franz Ferdinand,' she said. 'We're due in Sarajevo in half an hour.'

A door-to-door salesman specializing in toilet articles arrived at a remote cottage in the country. He tried in vain to make a sale but the woman at the door was obviously reluctant to spend any money. Finally the salesman said, 'Well, how about this — it's our latest line — a lavatory brush. Excellent quality.' This seemed to interest the woman and, to the salesman's delight, she bought one.

A few months later, he was passing the same cottage and he knocked on the door and asked the woman whether she had found the lavatory brush satisfactory. 'Oh, yes,' she said. 'I like it very much. But my husband's a bit old-fashioned, you know. He still prefers toilet paper.'

A small boy was taken to see an exhibition of abstract art at the Tate Gallery. His mother pointed to one painting and said, 'That is supposed to be a man on a horse.'

And the little boy said, 'Well, why isn't it?'

A fellow went in to see a psychiatrist and the doctor said, 'What seems to be the problem?'

'Oh, there's nothing wrong with me,' said the man. 'I'm Napoleon. It's my wife, Josephine. She thinks she's Mrs Brown.'

One Saturday afternoon, there was a commotion on the golf course as a young lady dressed in a resplendent wedding-gown stormed on to the green, strode over to a young golfer, and screamed, 'You miserable, no-good bastard! Do you know what time it is?'

The young golfer looked up from his putt and said, 'But Sylvia, I told you – only if it was raining!'

At a recent school nativity play near London, three six-year-olds were playing the part of the kings. During the scene in the stable, the first stepped forward with his gift and said, 'Gold.' The second stepped forward and said, 'Myrrh.' Then the third stepped forward and said, 'And Frank sent this.'

Two schoolboys at Eton became bitter enemies. When they left school, one went into the Church and the other into the Navy. The years passed and the first boy became a bishop, while the second attained the rank of admiral.

One day, the bishop, now grown fat, was standing on platform seven at Paddington station when he caught sight of his old enemy, resplendent in full admiral's uniform. 'I say, porter,' he said with a sly smile, 'is this the right platform for Oxford?'

'It is, madam,' said the admiral without batting an eye, 'but do you think you should be travelling in your condition?'

On a long-distance British Airways flight to Australia, a mother took her young son to the toilet and told him she would come back for him in five minutes. However, he was finished in two minutes so he left the toilet and wandered off down the aisle in the opposite direction to where his mother was sitting so she didn't notice.

Meanwhile, a businessman entered the toilet and locked the door. After the five minutes were up, the mother went to the toilet, knocked on the door and called out, 'Do you need any help with your zipper?'

From behind the door, a startled male voice said, 'Good God, that's what I call service!'

A well-known actor landed the lead in a smash hit West End musical. With the prospect of a long run at a fabulous salary, he decided to have his apartment redecorated from top to bottom, and engaged a painter and decorator for the job. In order to get off on the right foot, he presented the decorator with a couple of expensive front-row tickets for the show.

At the end of the first month he received a bill from the decorator, for the first four weeks' work. One of the items read: *4 hours overtime watching customer sing and dance.*

Two Frenchmen were arguing over the precise meaning of the word 'savoir-faire'. Pierre said, 'If you're making love to another man's wife and the husband bursts in and catches you at it and says, "Go ahead", that's "savoir-faire".'

'No, no,' said Jean-Paul. 'If the husband bursts in and says "Go ahead", and you *do* go ahead – *that's* "savoir-faire"!'

A salesman walked up to a house one morning and saw a little boy playing on the front step. 'Hello, sonny,' he said. 'Is your mother in?'

'Yes,' said the little lad, so the salesman knocked on the door. There was no reply, so he knocked again and waited patiently. No one answered his knock, so he turned to the little boy and said, 'I thought you said your mother was in?'

'She is,' said the lad. 'But we don't live here.'

A young fellow laboured under the delusion that he was a Yorkshire terrier. His friends persuaded him to seek professional help and he went to a psychiatrist for a course of treatment. Some weeks later, he met one of his friends in the street. 'And how are things now?' asked his friend. 'Did the psychiatrist cure you?'

'Oh, yes,' said the young fellow. 'I'm quite OK now. Fit as a fiddle – here, feel my nose.'

The vicar glanced out of his study window and saw Mrs Robinson coming up the garden path. Now Mrs Robinson was a terrible bore, so he rushed upstairs to his

bedroom and left his wife to entertain the unwelcome guest.

Half an hour later, he tiptoed out on to the landing and hearing no sound from the living-room, he called down, 'Has that horrible old bore gone yet, dear?'

With admirable presence of mind, his wife called back, 'Yes, dear, she went ages ago. Mrs Robinson is here now.'

A young married couple decided they needed an au pair and arranged for a girl to come over from northern Finland. When she arrived, the wife asked, 'Can you cook?'

'No,' said the Finnish girl. 'My mother always did the cooking.'

'Can you do the housework?' asked the wife.

'No,' said the girl. 'My older sister always did the housework.'

'Well, then,' said the wife, 'you'd better just look after the children.'

'I don't know how to do that,' said the girl. 'My younger sister always took care of the children in our family.'

The wife looked at her husband in despair. 'What can you do then?' she asked.

'Well,' said the Finnish girl brightly, 'I can milk reindeer.'

A fellow tried to get on a British Airways flight with a little Yorkshire terrier in his arms. The stewardess told him that dogs were not allowed on board so he went to the airport shop and bought himself a pair of dark glasses and a white walking-stick. This time he was greeted by another stewardess who said, 'It's quite unusual to see a Yorkshire terrier as a guide dog, sir. They're usually Golden Labradors.'

'You mean this isn't a Golden Labrador!' said the man in surprise.

A blind golfer once challenged a well-known professional to a game. 'But that would be taking an unfair advantage of you,' protested the pro.

'Not at all,' said the blind man. 'And furthermore, I'll play you for £50 a hole.'

'Well, if you insist,' said the pro. 'When would you like to play?'

'Any night,' said the blind man. 'Any night at all.'

The Queen was visiting a remote Scottish town when she was introduced to a man, his wife and his twelve children. 'Are all of these your children?' she asked, and the man said, 'Yes, they are, Your Majesty.'

'Good gracious!' said the Queen. 'We ought to give you a knighthood!'

'He's got one,' said the wife. 'But he refuses to wear it!'

Two African big game hunters were having lunch in their club. They became engaged in a heated argument and one of them said, 'I'm absolutely certain, old boy, that the word is spelled "w-h-o-o-m-b".'

'Nonsense, old chap,' protested the other. 'It's spelled "w-o-o-m".'

A waitress who just happened to be passing said, 'Excuse

me, gentlemen, I couldn't help overhearing. I think the word is spelled "w-o-m-b".'

One of the hunters turned to the other and said, 'It's obvious, old boy, that this young lady has never heard a bull elephant fart.'

A young lady had just emerged from a hot bath when the doorbell rang. Dripping wet, she ran to the door and called out, 'I can't let you in – I've just got out of the bath.'

'That's all right, lady,' said a voice from the other side of the door. 'I'm a blind salesman.'

'All right, then,' said the young lady and she opened the door.

'Thanks,' said the man. 'Where shall I put the blinds?'

A fellow visiting a small town in a remote area of Ireland wandered into the local snooker hall one evening in search of a game. He was shown to the only table in the place, which was very much the worse for wear. Not only that, there was only one broken-down old cue, and the balls were all of the same, dirty-grey colour. 'I can't play with these!' he protested. 'How am I supposed to tell the reds from the white?'

'It's OK, sir,' said the manager. 'You'll get to know them by their shape.'

Hearing that London Zoo was in danger of closing down, an Irish visitor to London decided to pay a visit. He stopped in front of the kangaroo cage and appeared to be fascinated by the animals. 'Do you have a special interest in these?' asked a passing attendant.

'I do that,' said the Irishman and pointed to a notice on the cage which read: A NATIVE OF AUSTRALIA. 'My sister married one!'

A well-known explorer set off for an expedition in New Guinea and was captured by a tribe of head-hunters. After some weeks he managed to escape and he immediately telephoned his wife to say he was safe. 'I need some clothes, dear,' he said. 'Will you send out a bush jacket, size 40 short, some tropical shirts, 16 collar, and a pair of strong shoes, size 8. Oh, and I need a hat.'

'What size hat?' his wife asked.

'One and seven-eighths.'

A young lady was talking to an astronomer at a party. 'I can understand how you people work out how far the stars are from the earth, and what their sizes are,' she said, 'but how on earth do you find out what their names are?'

At the start of the Irish racing season, a horsebox arrived at one of the courses, and when the stable lads opened the doors, they found that the box was empty. 'Well,' said the driver in explanation, '*somebody* has to bring the non-runners!'

A soldier serving overseas received a photograph from his girlfriend which showed two couples arm in arm while she sat alone to one side. In the accompanying letter she explained that she was being very good and saving herself only for him. Delighted, he showed the photograph and the letter to a friend. His pal studied them carefully and then said, 'Yes, but who took the picture?'

An MP was visiting Moscow on a fact-finding tour and he discovered that he was expected to make a speech. He decided to deliver his address in Russian so he had a Russian-speaking member of the British Embassy draw up a short speech and then learned it phonetically. On his way to deliver his address, he remembered that he had forgotten to find out the Russian for 'Ladies and Gentlemen' as his introduction. Just then, he passed a public convenience so he stopped the car and made a note of the Russian words over the entrance.

At the dinner, he rose to give his address and was very surprised that his opening words were greeted with gales of laughter. The rest of his speech went quite well, and afterwards, he asked his friend at the British Embassy, who had also been present, why everyone had laughed so much when he started speaking. 'Well,' said his friend, 'it might have been that you started off with "Male and female urinals".'

A Londoner decided to try a pony-trekking holiday for a change, though he had never ridden in his life and knew nothing about ponies or horses. As he was preparing to set off in the stable yard on the first morning, the instructor said, 'Excuse me – you're putting the saddle on backwards.'

'Oh yeah?' said the novice. 'And 'ow do you know which way I'm going to go?'

It was the first day at the new school and the children had been instructed to bring in their birth certificates for the school records. Four-year-old Janet came home that afternoon in tears. 'What's the matter, dear?' her mother asked.

And little Janet sobbed, 'I've lost my excuse for being born!'

Two married couples went away on holiday together to Spain. At the end of the first week, they were bored to tears, and one of the husbands suggested that they swap partners to try and liven things up a bit. They all agreed it was worth a try. The following morning, the husband who had suggested the exchange said, 'I'm glad we tried this. It was fun. Let's go and see how the girls got on.'

An explorer was walking through the jungle when he came across a poisonous snake. He walked cautiously round it and then he noticed that it wasn't a snake at all but a stick. 'I was absolutely terrified,' he told a friend that evening.

'But if it was only a stick,' said his friend, 'why were you terrified?'

'Because,' said the explorer, 'the stick I picked up to hit it with *was* a snake!'

Bill had been married for fifteen years and one night he took a friend home to dinner. As they entered the house, Bill's wife came running up to him, threw her arms round his neck, and kissed him affectionately.

'You're a lucky guy, Bill,' said his friend. 'Married for fifteen years and you still get a welcome like that when you come home.'

'It doesn't mean a thing,' said Bill. 'She only does it to make the dog jealous.'

The Archbishop of Canterbury was making his first visit to New York. His advisers suggested that he should be very diplomatic and tactful in answering questions from press and TV reporters, so as to avoid any controversy. There was a huge crowd of reporters waiting to greet him and, as he stepped from the plane, one of them thrust a microphone in his face and said, 'Say, Bishop, what's your opinion of the large number of brothels in Manhattan?'

Remembering that he had to be tactful, and suffering slightly from jet-lag, the Archbishop said cautiously, 'Are there any brothels in Manhattan?'

The following morning, the headlines of the *New York Times* read: ARCHBISHOP'S FIRST QUESTION ON ARRIVING IN NEW YORK – 'ARE THERE ANY BROTHELS IN MANHATTAN?'

The mother of a teenage boy was asked by his headmaster to call in at his office to discuss a serious matter. When she arrived, the headmaster said, 'I'm sorry to have to tell you that your son came to school yesterday wearing a print dress, high-heeled court shoes and lipstick!'

'Damn it!' said the boy's mother. 'I've told him a hundred times not to wear his father's clothes!'

Two photography enthusiasts were discussing their day at a bar in Barcelona. 'I saw an old beggar this morning,' said one, 'down on the Ramblas. He was wearing filthy rags, and he looked really ill and desperate.'

'Poor chap,' sympathized his pal. 'What did you give him?'

'Well, the light was pretty good so I gave him f-16 at 1/100.'

The year was 1916. Captain Fotheringham of the Royal Flying Corps had just shot down the German air ace Baron von Hohingen over the English lines. The Baron had survived the crash and Captain Fotheringham went to visit him in hospital. 'Is there anything I can do for you, old boy?' he asked.

'Yes, there is,' said the Baron. 'They are going to amputate my left leg. Would you drop it over Germany for me?'

'Leave it to me, old bean,' said Captain Fotheringham, and that very day he carried out the request.

A week later, he returned to the hospital for another visit and this time the German said, 'May I ask you another favour? They are going to remove my right leg. Once again, would you drop it over the Fatherland?'

So once again, Fotheringham carried out the strange request, and the following day he paid a further visit to the hospital. 'Captain,' said von Hohingen, 'this afternoon, they are going to remove my right arm. Once again, could I ask you to drop it behind the German lines?'

'Of course, old chap,' said Captain Fotheringham thoughtfully. 'But I say, look here, you're not trying to escape, are you?'

'I've got an infallible betting system for the races,' said Smithers. 'I just think of something that has happened to me recently, and then I look for a horse that fits. I'll give you an example. A couple of weeks ago, I dropped the teapot – so I backed "Broken China" and it romped home at twenty to one. Then the day after I had been playing roulette at the casino, I backed "Wheel of Fortune" – it won. Last Christmas, we went to the pantomime, so I backed "Cinderella" at a hundred to eight and it came in second – I cleared £250.'

'Sounds good to me,' said Brown. 'I'll try it.'

When they met in the pub a week later, Smithers said, 'How did you get on with my betting system?'

'Didn't work for me,' said Brown. 'I was walking to work yesterday and my hat blew off. The nearest horse I could find was "Winds of Change".'

'And did it win?' asked Smithers.

'Came in last,' said Brown. 'The winner was some French horse called "Mon Chapeau".'

In an effort to boost sales, British Airways announced that for two weeks only, any business executive who travelled on a midweek flight could take his wife along with him for only twenty per cent of the normal fare. In order to judge the success of this experiment, they wrote to all the wives concerned, asking them if they had enjoyed their flights. Eighty-five per cent of the wives wrote back asking, 'What flight?'

An American visiting England started to chat up a pretty young thing in a bar. 'You know,' he said conversationally, 'I come from the other side.'

'Let's go home at once,' said the girl, finishing her drink quickly. 'This I've got to see!'

'I had a funny old dream last night,' a chap in the local said to his pal. 'I dreamed I went to Dreamland at Margate and had a wonderful time on the roller coaster.'

'I had a dream last night too,' said his friend. 'I dreamed I was alone in my room with Madonna! And then the door opened and in walked Michelle Pfeiffer and Julia Roberts!'

'Well, you're a fine one,' said the first fellow. 'Why didn't you telephone me?'

'I did,' said his pal. 'But your wife told me you'd gone to Margate.'

One afternoon, the telephone rang in the doctor's surgery. It was the young lady he had been examining that morning. 'Would you mind having a look round your office, doctor?' she said. 'I think I left my panties there.'

The doctor had a good look round his office and then said, 'I'm sorry but they don't seem to be here.'

'Oh, well,' said the young lady, 'never mind. I suppose I must have left them at the dentist's.'

A trombone player was rehearsing late at night in his room when there was a knock on the door. He opened it to find an irate neighbour who said, 'Hey! Do you know there's a little old lady sick next door?'

'No,' said the musician. 'But if you hum a few bars, I'll improvise.'

The boss was extremely annoyed when his secretary made a couple of corrections in a letter he had dictated. 'You're not paid to correct my work,' he stormed. 'Just type it out exactly as I dictated it – no corrections, no additions, no deletions.'

The next letter that his secretary produced for signature read as follows:

DEAR MR DEAN
– I don't know whether the idiot spells it with an e on the end – you can look it up – in reply to your letter of the – where the hell's that letter – oh, well, look it up yourself – the price you quote is far too high – greedy old sod! – and we would suggest a figure nearer to our initial estimate – estimate, huh! – blind guess would be nearer the mark – we await your comments – and if you don't like it you can lump it! – usual bumph at the end – and isn't it about time for a coffee?

On the day before the Battle of Hastings, King Harold said to his commander of the army, 'Are the troops all ready?'

'They are, Your Majesty,' said the commander. 'Would you like a demonstration?'

'Yes, I would,' said the king. So the commander lined all the archers up and instructed them to fire off a volley. Three thousand arrows sped through the air and landed a quarter of a mile away. But one clumsy archer fired straight up into the air, and the arrow went up several hundred feet, turned round and came back down again, landing about six inches from where the king was standing.

'You want to watch that fellow,' said the king. 'If he's not careful, he'll have somebody's eye out tomorrow!'

A French diplomat was on a visit to London, and his host, an MP, took him round all the sights and gave him a good time. On the last day of his visit, the Frenchman was asked if he would like to pay a visit to the House of Commons. 'It is very kind of you,' he said, 'but I must not cockroach on your time any further.'

'That's all right,' said the MP. 'But I hope you won't mind my pointing it out — the word is "encroach" not "cockroach".'

'Ah, I see,' replied the Frenchman. 'It is a question of gender!'

The famous millionaire John D. Rockefeller had a very strict upbringing. Discipline in the Rockefeller household was severe in the extreme. On one occasion, he was receiving a caning from his mother, during the course of which he managed to convince her that he was not guilty of the offence for which he was being punished.

'Very well,' said his mother. 'But we have gone so far that we may as well proceed. It will be credited to your account for next time.'

A missionary in Africa came upon a witch doctor pounding away at a large drum. 'What are you doing?' asked the missionary.

'We have no water,' said the witch doctor.

'I see,' said the missionary. 'So I suppose you're praying for rain?'

'No,' said the witch doctor. 'I'm calling the plumber.'

A man was walking along the banks of a canal when he noticed a chap struggling in the water. 'What's your name?' he shouted.

'Alf Brown,' the man in the water shouted back. 'But get me out of here – I'm drowning!'

'Where do you work?' shouted the man on the bank.

'At the coal mine down the road!'

The fellow on the bank immediately walked off and presented himself to the manager of the coal mine. 'Do you have an Alf Brown working here?' he asked.

'We do,' said the manager.

'Well, I've come for his job – he's just drowned in the canal.'

'You're too late,' said the manager. 'The fellow that pushed him in has got it.'

'How old are you, Grandma?' asked little Samantha. 'Oh, I don't know, dear,' said Grandma with a smile. 'I've had so many birthdays, I've lost count!'

'Well, why don't you look in your knickers,' said Samantha. 'Mine say three to four years old.'

A well-known duke used to take breakfast in bed at his country estate and one morning a new maid came in with the breakfast tray. She was very young and pretty and the duke said, 'Good morning, my dear. You're new, aren't you?'

'Yes, sir,' said the maid as she put down the tray.

'You're a pretty little thing,' said the duke. 'Come and sit here on the bed.'

'Yes, sir,' said the girl and she sat down on the bed.

'You must learn the correct way to address me,' said the duke. 'Now, first of all, you must say "Your Grace".'

So the girl got down on her knees at the side of the bed and said, 'For what I am about to receive, may the Lord make me truly thankful.'

An angler returned from a day on the river, carrying the biggest fish the club had ever seen. It was fully three feet long and was obviously a record-breaker. His bitterest rival in the angling club came in shortly afterwards carrying three or four tiny fishes on a string. The first fisherman smiled and pointed silently at his monster catch. The second angler looked at it for a few moments and then said, 'Just caught the one, I see.'

A couple of American golfing enthusiasts came over on a visit and went up to St Andrews for a game. 'What's the course fee?' they asked the secretary.

'As you're American visitors,' he said, 'there'll be no charge.'

'Gee, that's swell,' said the Americans. 'Could we hire some clubs?'

'Certainly,' said the secretary. 'Help yourself – there'll be nothing to pay.'

Delighted, the Americans said, 'And could we have some balls?'

'Of course,' said the secretary, handing over a set. 'That'll be £150.'

The Americans paid up and as they walked off to the first tee, one of them said, 'These Limeys! When they grab you, they certainly know where to do it!'

A strong supporter of the Women's Liberation movement was holding a committee meeting in her house. 'We have some guests with us tonight,' she said. 'I'd like you all to welcome Mr and Mrs Forbes-Robertson.' Then, remembering where she was, she added, 'Not necessarily in that order, of course!'

A little girl wandered into the bathroom whilst her mother was taking a bath and said, 'Mummy – why is your tummy so big?'

'Well, you see,' said her mother, 'Daddy has given me a baby.'

Downstairs later on, the little girl said to her father, 'Daddy, did you give Mummy a little baby?'

'Yes, I did,' said Daddy, smiling.

'Well,' said the little girl, 'I think she's eaten it!'

A travelling salesman found himself stranded in a small village one winter's night. He knocked on the door of a farmhouse and asked the farmer if he would put him up for the night. 'All right,' said the farmer, 'as long as you don't mind sharing a room with my young son.'

'My God!' said the salesman. 'I'm in the wrong joke!'

The orchestra had just finished playing Tchaikovsky's *Nutcracker Suite*. A lady in the third row of the stalls turned to her husband and said, 'I do hope they're going to play Tchaikovsky's *Nutcracker Suite*.'

'They've just finished playing it!' said her husband.

'Well, you might have told me!' said the matron. 'It's my favourite piece!'

A fellow who had great difficulty getting to sleep at night went to see his doctor. The doctor prescribed some sleeping pills and that night he took a pill and fell asleep as soon as his head touched the pillow. He woke feeling completely refreshed, bright and alive, and went off to work with a spring in his step.

Walking into the office he said to his boss, 'You'll be glad to know I had no trouble getting to sleep last night and I woke up this morning even before the alarm went off.'

'That's great,' said his boss. 'But where were you yesterday?'

A representative for a publishing firm plodded round his territory for months without making a single sale. He began to grow desperate. He couldn't keep up his mortgage payments, his wife had to take a job, and the bills were mounting up. Finally, after eight months, he made his first sale – and then realized that he'd forgotten the name of the firm he was working for.

A maid had been employed by the same family for several years. One day she told her mistress that she would have to leave because she was pregnant. 'Well,' said her mistress, 'as you have no husband, and rather than lose you, we'll adopt the child.'

A year later, the maid again found herself pregnant, and once again, her mistress agreed to adopt the baby rather than lose her services.

Twelve months later, the maid was pregnant again, and once more her mistress offered to adopt the child. 'No, I'm definitely leaving this time,' said the maid. 'I couldn't work for a family that has three children.'

A fellow was waiting in a doctor's reception when a young girl came out of the surgery sobbing bitterly. 'What's the matter?' he asked sympathetically.

'The doctor's just told me I'm pregnant,' she said.

It was the fellow's turn next and when he went into the doctor's surgery, he said, 'Is that young lady really pregnant?'

'No,' said the doctor, 'but it's cured her hiccups.'

A confirmed atheist was visiting the house of a vicar. He noticed a very beautiful gold and silver model of the solar system with a globe representing the earth, surrounded by all the planets. 'I'd love one of those,' said the atheist. 'Who made it?'

'Oh, nobody made it,' said the vicar. 'It just happened.'

A chap was driving through Ireland on holiday when he came across a pile of stones with a red light on top of it in the middle of the road. He pulled up just in time and asked a farmer who was leaning over a nearby gate what the light was for. 'It's to keep motorists from running into the pile of stones, of course,' said the farmer.

'But what are the stones for?' asked the motorist.

'Why, to put the light on,' said the farmer.

A man on holiday in Las Vegas lost all his money at the tables. He went up to a rich Texan at the bar and said, 'Would you lend me $100 – I think my luck's turning and I'll be able to pay you back in no time.' The Texan generously lent him $100 and the fellow went back to the roulette wheel where he lost the lot in five minutes.

The next evening, he again managed to borrow $100 from the rich Texan, and once again he lost it all at the roulette wheel. This continued every night for a week. And then, one evening in the bar, the unlucky punter told his best friend all about it and asked him what he'd advise. 'There's only one thing you can do,' said his friend. 'Stay away from the bum! He's bad luck for you!'

An angler was regaling his friends with tales of the day's fishing. 'I ran short of bait this morning,' he said, 'but when I glanced down, I noticed a small snake with a frog in its mouth. I removed the frog and cut it up for bait. Feeling sorry for depriving the snake of its lunch, I took out my hip flask and gave it a nip of whisky. The snake glided off and I went back to my rod. About half an hour later, I felt something against my boot. I looked down — and there was the same snake with three more frogs.'

A fellow applied for a job and the personnel manager said, 'I'm sorry but I can't help you. What with the recession, we're over-staffed as it is — there just isn't enough work to go round.'

'That's all right,' said the applicant. 'The little bit of work I would do wouldn't be noticed.'

An insurance salesman was trying to sell a policy to a factory owner. 'I've got all the insurance I need,' said the executive. 'Fire, accident, employer's liability, the lot, so don't waste your time.'

'Are you covered against floods?' asked the salesman.

'Floods?' said the businessman with interest. 'How do you arrange a flood?'

A so-called New Evangelist was travelling round the country preaching the gospel. He put up for the night at a small hotel and after he had got settled into his room, he

called down to the pretty blonde receptionist and asked her to come up to his room, as soon as she finished work. Out of curiosity she did so and was amazed, when she entered his room at about 11 o'clock, to find him undressed and in bed. 'Get in, my dear,' he said, holding back the bedclothes for her.

'But I thought you were a man of God!' she said, slightly bewildered.

'It's quite all right, my dear,' said the preacher. 'There's nothing wrong in it – it's written in the Bible.'

Somewhat reassured, she undressed and got into bed and they made love several times through the night. Every time she expressed doubts about what they were doing, the preacher calmed her fears by saying, 'It's written in the Bible.'

The next day, after he had left, she went up to his room to try to find out exactly where it was 'written in the Bible'. Opening the Gideon Bible on the bedside table, she saw inscribed on the flyleaf the words: 'The blonde receptionist is a very good screw.'

There had been severe flooding throughout the West Country and the vicar was stranded on the roof of the church. A rowing boat passed close by and one of the rowers shouted, 'Come on down, vicar – get in the boat!'

'Save the others!' the vicar shouted. 'The Lord will save me!'

The waters continued to rise and just as they reached the vicar's waist, a motor boat chugged up. Again the vicar cried, 'Save the others! The Lord will save me!'

The motor boat chugged off and an hour passed. By the time the helicopter arrived, the water was up to the vicar's chin. 'Hang on!' shouted the helicopter pilot. 'We'll lower a rope!'

'No, no!' shouted the vicar. 'The Lord will save me!'

As the helicopter flew off, the waters rose still further and the vicar disappeared from view. When he arrived in Heaven, he said indignantly to God, 'Oh Lord – why did you let me down? I was sure you would save me!'

'What do you mean – let you down?' said God. 'I sent two boats and a helicopter to take you off that roof, didn't I?'

The world's most brilliant salesman once managed to sell a refrigerator to an Eskimo. Some months later, he called round again to see how the Eskimo was getting on with his new purchase. 'OK,' said the Eskimo, 'but I haven't quite got the knack of chopping up the ice into little squares to fit the tray.'

A young lady was regaling her friends with intimate details about her honeymoon. 'As soon as we got to the hotel,' she said, 'Roger rushed me up to the room, undressed us both, and we had a performance. Then just before dinner we had another performance. After dinner, we went upstairs and had another performance. During the night he woke me up three times and we had a performance each time. Then just before breakfast we had a dress rehearsal.'

'What's a dress rehearsal?' asked one of her friends.

'It's the same as a performance,' said the young lady, 'but nobody comes.'

Some time towards the end of the eighteenth century, an Englishman and an Italian quarrelled. Neither of them wanted to fight a duel, but their friend persuaded them that this was the only right thing to do. It was agreed that they would fight with pistols, alone in a darkened room. The candles were put out, and the Englishman, not wishing to harm the Italian, fired up the chimney – and hit the Italian in the backside.

During a heavy raid on London at the height of the Blitz, an air-raid warden shouted down from the entrance to a shelter, 'Are there any expectant mothers down there?'

'It's hard to say,' shouted a female voice. 'We've only been down here ten minutes!'

A woman walked into a psychiatrist's office carrying a duck under her arm. 'What seems to be the problem?' asked the psychiatrist.

'Well, it's not me, actually,' said the woman. 'It's my husband. He thinks he's a duck.'

'I understand you're a doctor,' said a lady at a cocktail party. 'I wonder if I could ask you a question? I've been getting these pains in my side and sometimes in my leg as well.'

'I'm sorry,' the man interrupted, 'I'm not that kind of doctor. I'm a Doctor of Economics.'

'Oh, I see,' said the lady. 'Well, in that case, should I sell my British Telecom shares?'

Moskowitz rang Goldstein to ask how business was going. 'Fine, fine,' said Goldstein. 'Even with the recession, sales are up fifteen per cent. I'm thinking of expanding into the overseas market. On top of that, my son, the doctor, has opened his own private practice and is making £200,000 a year. And my daughter, the lawyer, has been made a senior partner in the firm, and has just won a big civil case with a fee of £50,000 . . .'

'I'll phone back later,' interrupted Moskowitz. 'I didn't realize you had someone with you.'

'And does anyone know where God lives?' asked the Sunday School teacher.

'In our bathroom,' said a little boy in the front row.

'What on earth makes you say that?' asked the teacher.

'Well,' replied the lad, 'every morning my Dad thumps on the door and shouts, "God, are you still in there!" '

The new member of the exclusive golf club was behaving very badly at dinner. He was obviously very drunk and cursed and swore continuously at the waiters. A senior committee member approached him and said, 'Look here, I am the Chairman of the Greens Committee . . .'

'Just the chap I want to see!' said the new member. 'These bloody sprouts are cold!'

The old man was dying and he called his wife and family to his bedside. There were four sons – three fine, big boys and a little one. He said to his wife in a weak voice, 'Don't lie to me now − I want to know the truth. The little one − is he really mine?'

'Oh, yes, dear,' said his wife. 'He really is − I give you my word of honour.'

The old man smiled and slipped peacefully away. With a sigh of relief, the widow muttered, 'Thank God he didn't ask me about the other three!'

A young English couple emigrated to America and went house-hunting in Alabama where they had decided to settle. The real estate agent showed them one house which appeared to be perfect and they clinched the deal there and then. When they got back to their hotel, they realized that they hadn't seen a WC in the house so they wrote to the agent and asked where the WC was located. Now of course in America, the term 'WC' is not used. The agent puzzled for a while and then came to the conclusion that they must mean 'Wesleyan Chapel'.

So he wrote back as follows: 'The WC is located about ten miles from the house. I realize this is rather a long way away, especially if you're in the habit of going regularly. However, it's well worth a visit − some folks take a picnic lunch and make a day of it. It's a fine old building and seats two hundred people. Next year, they're thinking of holding a raffle to raise funds to instal plush seats. I often wish I could go more often myself, but perhaps we'll meet up there some time.'

Two business executives were dining in an expensive restaurant. One of them called the waiter over and said, 'Could you lend us a 10p piece — we want to settle a bet.' The waiter handed over the coin, which was duly flipped, and the bet settled. When the waiter brought the bill, the final item read: *Loan of 10p piece — £1.50.*

Father was reading the paper one evening when his small son came in and said, 'Daddy, will you take me to the zoo tomorrow?'

'No,' his father answered. 'If the zoo wants you, let them come and get you.'

An American soldier in wartime London was telling the customers in a bar about his impressions of England. 'This country's wide open!' he enthused. 'A guy can get anything he wants for a pack of cigarettes and some gum!'

Two rather refined English brothers were listening. One of them was rather deaf and he turned to the other and asked, 'What's he saying?'

'He says he likes England,' said the other.

'And those English broads!' the American continued. 'They're game for anything! Just give them the nod and they're away!'

'What's he saying?' said the deaf brother.

'He says he likes English women,' said the other.

'Take last night,' continued the American. 'I met up with this rich old broad, and before I knew it, I was back in her apartment! She sank a bottle of Scotch in no time flat — then she ripped off her clothes, dragged me into the bedroom, and we were at it all night!'

'What's he saying?' asked the deaf brother.

And the other brother replied, 'He says he's met Mother.'

There are two gates into Heaven. One has a sign saying: QUEUE HERE ALL MEN WHO ARE *NOT* HENPECKED BY THEIR WIVES. The other gate has a sign saying: QUEUE HERE ALL MEN WHO *ARE* HENPECKED BY THEIR WIVES.

Reporting for duty one morning, St Peter saw a long line of men queuing up by the second gate, and one small, meek-looking man standing by the first gate. He asked the little man what his qualifications were for standing by the gate with the sign saying: QUEUE HERE ALL MEN WHO ARE *NOT* HENPECKED BY THEIR WIVES.

'I don't know really,' said the man. 'My wife told me to come and queue here.'

A very rich lady visited her favourite designer and said, 'I need a new hat – something glamorous and startling, yet simple in design.' Jean-Paul pulled out a length of beautiful ribbon and began to cut and fold it. In five minutes he had produced a beautiful and original hat.

'That will be £500, madame,' he said.

'£500!' said the lady. 'That's an outrageous price for a simple length of ribbon!'

Without a word, Jean-Paul unwound the ribbon and dismantled the hat. Handing the ribbon to the lady, he said quietly, 'The ribbon itself, madame, is yours for nothing.'

A young business executive from Hong Kong came over to England for a holiday. He met an attractive young lady and invited her to come back with him to Hong Kong – as his wife, of course – all fair and above board. She willingly agreed, and after the wedding in London, they flew back to the Far East.

On the first morning after their return, the husband had to leave early for the office, so he got out of bed quietly and left without waking his wife. A few minutes later, the Chinese servant came into the bedroom and shook the young bride's shoulder. 'Come along, missy,' he said. 'Time to get dressed and go home!'

A young Spanish girl married the handsomest man in the village and on their wedding night she was pleasantly surprised by his vigour and manhood. 'Oh, Miguel,' she cried. 'You are so magnificently endowed!'

'Yes,' said Miguel proudly, 'and I alone in the whole village have such prodigious equipment!'

After a few weeks, Miguel had to go away for a couple of weeks for the sheep-shearing. When he returned, his bride met him at the door and said angrily, 'Miguel, you lied to me! You said you alone in the whole village were so magnificently endowed but it is not true! Don Antonio also has one just as good as yours!'

Miguel thought quickly. 'Ah, I forgot to tell you!' he said. 'You see, I had two – and I gave one to my friend, Don Antonio.'

'You fool!' screamed his wife. 'You gave him the best one!'

A rabbi, a Protestant minister, a Catholic priest and a Baptist preacher were discussing religion. The rabbi said, 'Let's be honest with each other. We all have our vices. For instance, I'm not supposed to eat ham or pork – but I love them!'

The Protestant minister said, 'Well, I do have one vice – I like my drink. In fact, I get really pissed from time to time.'

The Catholic priest said, 'I'll be honest. I like girls. I like to get laid at least once a week.'

They looked at the Baptist preacher. 'Haven't you got any vices?' they asked.

'Well, only one,' he said. 'I like to gossip!'

The village policeman was about to retire. He had been in the village for thirty years and was just about the most unpopular figure there. It was his proud boast that he had booked every resident in the village at some time or another, usually for some very minor infringement. The only man he had never been able to catch out was the local vicar, and he determined to rectify this omission before his retirement became due. The task seemed hopeless but as he watched the vicar cycling by one day, he hit upon a plan. He hid in some bushes at the bottom of a steep hill just outside the village and waited for the vicar to come cycling down. His plan was to dash out just at the last moment so that the vicar would run over his foot and he could have him for riding with faulty brakes.

He waited for over an hour but then at last the vicar came pedalling down the hill. As he drew near, the policeman dashed out from the bushes – but the vicar's reflexes were good and he pulled up about three inches from the constable's foot. 'Well,' said the policeman, 'I thought I had you there, vicar, I really did.'

'Ah, yes, but you see,' said the vicar, smiling, 'God was with me!'

'Got you at last!' said the bobbie. 'Two on a bike!'

Young Jimmy Smith was called into the headmaster's office because his teacher had reported him for using bad language. 'What exactly did you say?' asked the headmaster.

'Oh, I couldn't use them words in front of you, sir!' said Jimmy.

'Jimmy, I want to know exactly what swear words you used.'

'Well, sir,' said Jimmy, 'if you tell me a few of the ones you use yourself, I'll tell you when you come to the ones I used.'

A very devout vicar got married to an attractive young lady. On their wedding night, she went up to their room first, in order to prepare herself, and he followed half an hour later. Entering the bedroom, he found his bride, attired in a sexy nightgown, lying seductively on the bed. 'I had hoped, my dear,' he said, 'to find you on your knees at the side of the bed.'

'Well, all right,' said his bride, 'if you want me to – but doing it that way, I always get the hiccups.'

A young medical student halfway through his course developed a sore throat. He decided he knew enough about medicine to write out his own prescription which he duly handed in at the chemist's. The chemist read it through carefully and then said doubtfully, 'Is it a very large dog, sir?'

The trial had been going on for three hours when the judge suddenly noticed that there were only eleven people in the jury box. 'Where is the twelfth man?' he asked the foreman of the jury.

'He had to go away on business,' said the foreman, 'but it's all right – he left his verdict with me.'

'I'm prescribing these pills for you,' said the doctor to the grossly overweight patient, who tipped the scales at about seventeen stone. 'I don't want you to swallow them. Just spill them on the floor twice a day and pick them up one at a time.'

A holidaymaker in America visited a Red Indian reservation and bought a peace pipe. He noticed some writing on the side of the pipe but the words were too small to make out. He turned to the Indian who had sold him the pipe and asked him what the words meant. The Indian examined it carefully, looked up, and said, 'It says, "Smoking can damage your health." '

It is reported that the old Duke of Gloucester once visited Cairo and was taken to see a display of belly-dancing. After the performance, he was taken round and introduced to the performer. There was a long silence while the Duke sought for some common ground on which to open the conversation. Finally he said, 'Do you know Tidworth?'

A group of hunters in the depths of an African forest decided to split up and meet back in the clearing three hours later. It was agreed that if any one of them got lost, he would shoot three times into the air to alert the others.

After about an hour, one member of the party found himself hopelessly lost so, as arranged, he shot three times into the air. Nothing happened, so he shot three times more. Again nobody came. 'I hope someone comes soon,' he muttered to himself, 'I've nearly run out of arrows.'

A married couple went away for a fortnight in the sun and arranged for their dog to be boarded in kennels. On their return, the husband went round and collected the dog and brought it home. 'I don't know what's got into Buster,' he said when he got in. 'He barked and struggled all the way home. I think he must be sickening for something.'

'It's not that,' said his wife. 'What he's been trying to tell you is that he's the wrong dog.'

A small boy returned home from his first day at school and proudly announced, 'We started maths today, Daddy.'

'Great,' said his father. 'What's one and one?'

'Er,' the little boy hesitated, 'we haven't got that far yet.'

It was a freezing cold day in the snow-covered steppes of Siberia. A young lad was walking along when he spotted a tiny bird being chased by a fox. The boy picked up the bird and, just at that moment, a horse came along and left a large deposit in the road. The boy scooped out a hole in the deposit and carefully placed the bird in it. It was warm and comfortable there and the bird soon recovered its spirits and poked its head out of the hole and began to sing with joy. But the hungry fox was still lurking nearby and it pounced on the little bird and gobbled it up.

The moral of this story is two-fold. First, it is not always your enemies who drop you in it. And, second, if you are up to your neck in it, keep your mouth shut!

There is a story about Dorothy Parker, the American wit, whose maid handed in her notice when she came in one day and found an alligator in the bath. She left the following note for Miss Parker: 'I cannot work in a house where there is an alligator in the bath. I would have mentioned this when I first took the job but I didn't think the matter would ever come up.'

More of the World's Best Drinking Jokes

Edward Phillips

You'll be well over the limit of humorous intake when you've finished this second hilarious cocktail of drinking jokes. A good measure of laughter is guaranteed!

Breaking with custom, a woman decided to have a Scotch and soda as a nightcap. After drinking it, she went upstairs to kiss her small son good night. After she had kissed him, he said, 'Mummy! You're wearing Daddy's perfume!'

Two friends were returning from a convivial evening at the local. 'Am I staggering at all?' asked one. 'If I am, the wife'll notice it and there'll be hell to pay. Hang on here a minute – I'll walk on ahead and you tell me if I'm walking straight.' He walked on a few steps and his mate said, 'You're all right – but the chap with you is staggering about all over the place.'

If you enjoy a tipple or two, you'll love this irresistible collection of *More of the World's Best Drinking Jokes*!

ISBN 0 00 637959 1

☐	WORLD'S BEST AFTER-DINNER JOKES Edward Phillips	0-00-637960-5	£2.99
☐	WORLD'S BEST SKIING JOKES Ernest Forbes	0-00-638246-0	£2.99
☐	WORLD'S BEST MOTORING JOKES Edward Phillips	0-00-638265-7	£2.99
☐	WORLD'S BEST BOSS JOKES Edward Phillips	0-00-638241-X	£2.99
☐	WORLD'S BEST DRINKING JOKES Ernest Forbes	0-00-638242-8	£2.99
☐	WORLD'S BEST DIRTY JOKES Mr J	0-00-637784-X	£2.99

These books are available from your local bookseller or can be ordered direct from the publishers.

To order direct just tick the titles you want and fill in the form below:

Name: _____

Address: _____

_____

Postcode: _____

Send to: HarperCollins Mail Order, Dept 8, HarperCollins*Publishers*, Westerhill Road, Bishopbriggs, Glasgow G64 2QT.

Please enclose a cheque or postal order or your authority to debit your Visa/Access account –

Credit card no: _____

Expiry date: _____

Signature: _____

– to the value of the cover price plus:

UK & BFPO: Add £1.00 for the first and 25p for each additional book ordered.

Overseas orders including Eire, please add £2.95 service charge.

Books will be sent by surface mail but quotes for airmail despatches will be given on request.

24 HOUR TELEPHONE ORDERING SERVICE FOR ACCESS/VISA CARDHOLDERS –
TEL: GLASGOW 041-772 2281 or LONDON 081-307 4052